T0193951

TOO MUCH OF THE HUMAN CONDITION

A Formula for Finding Your Essence
With The Human Growth Process
And a Unified Theory of the Self

NANCY S.B. GING, LCSW

BALBOA.
PRESS
A DIVISION OF HAY HOUSE

Interior Graphics/Art Credit: Nancy Ging; Kevin Ging

Balboa Press books may be ordered through booksellers or by contacting:

Balboa Press
A Division of Hay House
1663 Liberty Drive
Bloomington, IN 47403
www.balboapress.com
1 (877) 407-4847

Because of the dynamic nature of the Internet, any web addresses or links contained in this book may have changed since publication and may no longer be valid. The views expressed in this work are solely those of the author and do not necessarily reflect the views of the publisher, and the publisher hereby disclaims any responsibility for them.

The author of this book does not dispense medical advice or prescribe the use of any technique as a form of treatment for physical, emotional, or medical problems without the advice of a physician, either directly or indirectly. The intent of the author is only to offer information of a general nature to help you in your quest for emotional and spiritual well-being. In the event you use any of the information in this book for yourself, which is your constitutional right, the author and the publisher assume no responsibility for your actions.

Any people depicted in stock imagery provided by Getty Images are models, and such images are being used for illustrative purposes only. Certain stock imagery © Getty Images.

Print information available on the last page.

ISBN: 978-1-9822-2860-6 (sc)
ISBN: 978-1-9822-2861-3 (hc)
ISBN: 978-1-9822-2864-4 (e)

Library of Congress Control Number: 2019906911

Balboa Press rev. date: 06/07/2019

AUTHOR'S PREVIOUS PUBLICATIONS

SIMPLIFYING THE ROAD TO WHOLENESS
Published by Xlibris (2001)

KNOWING WHOLENESS
Through Poetry and Imagery
Published by Balboa (2016)

CONTENTS

ACKNOWLEDGEMENTS

With on-going gratitude for the grace, wisdom and practical skills of my assistant, Christine Romy, and support from Deb Bolden, L. Robin Condro, Karen Gernaey, Sue Levins, Susan Lincoln, and Kryshia Schwab.

DEDICATIONS

To my children, Tracey and Kevin, and
their offspring, Jade and Riley

and

To each person who has been like a rainbow
in my life, helping to move me forward to the
next level of awareness of the wholeness that
has, to my surprise, been there all along.

CHAPTER ONE
The Road Toward Liberation

Let us simplify. We need to simplify not because we are not smart. In fact, we are far wiser within our deepest Self than we would believe. Why must we simplify? Because living in the 21st century has become enormously complex and often bewildering. In our bewildering confusion and frequently overwhelmed state of mind, we often reach out for help, a wise step in the process of self-care. Finding support or assistance is something we all need at various times throughout our lives. Eleanor Roosevelt has said, "We are called to do that which we cannot do alone." Reaching out for connection is a basic human need. Finding help is not the problem.

Helpful professionals are plentiful and come in a variety of flavors with numerous types of credentials, various degrees of training and experience. Here is my concern and reason for this book: the behavioral sciences have created enormous complexity often causing people, even our psychotherapists and counselors, to lose sight of what is *most essential*. We want to grow, heal and evolve, but the very places we turn to for help with this growth may lead us astray with too much information, too many techniques. It is time to *expand* our consciousness while at the same time *reduce* the complexity in how we think about ourselves and our lives. Clients sometimes refer to me as their "shrink" to which I generally reply, "I'm not a 'shrink'. I am an expander of consciousness." However, in the material I put forth in this small book, I hope to shrink the complexity of helpful techniques and theories down to those which are most essential: *Essentials for the Human Growth Process*™ as I've defined and described it herein. Once the essentials are taken in, integrated in such a way that we can easily remember them, we can add whatever techniques and complexities we wish. However, let us keep it simple for starters and put the formula into *an easy to remember code:*

1-2-3, A-B-C

Apologies for the gimmicky sound of this, but these two trios of numbers and letters are an easy way to remember and use the essentials. Without a simple formula to hold on to, we can easily forget where we want to grow toward and get to. I have been to workshops over the years where it was suggested that we put signs up in our homes saying "Remember." Remember who you really are. This is good. Nice and simple. Yet who we are has more than one dimension. The formula in this book can help us remember all that we are at both the level of our human nature AND the level of our greater Self which is our Essence.

I would like to offer some practical perspectives which I've arrived at during the past 35 years in private practice as a holistic psychotherapist working with individuals, couples, and whole family systems. These approaches to wellness may sometimes feel spiritual as they lead us into our wholeness. However, these perspectives are not religious positions; yet they are compatible with all religions, all traditions, including agnostic, atheist individuals and hard scientists. This formula is for growing into true integration, integrity. At our deepest level we long to experience our wholeness. We have an urge to evolve and grow that is both psychological and spiritual.

This book is written for self-helpers, any individuals seeking **A**wareness, **B**alance, **C**ohesiveness—harmony and well-being on any and all levels. It is also written for counselors. We all are counselors at heart, and we all are wanting to know our own wholeness. We are all in this together, so this book is for all.

For counselors and clinicians working in agencies, the ideas presently herein should not be problematic for they deal with REALITY, Ultimate Reality. Theologian Paul Tillich's term, Ultimate Reality showed up for me when I was in the darkest chapter of my life. I was 28 years old, a time that some call the first Saturn Return. It can be one of life's most dramatic and challenging time periods. It certainly was a chaotic, unhinged time for me as I fell into deep depression.

Ultimate Reality and the rest of what I share herein is my cosmology, a world view which includes findings about the heart, the brain, the New Sciences, and some ideas which have occurred to me as I have done a dance of synthesizing many fields – biological, psychological, theological, religious, metaphysical – that have been useful to me in my own personal journey as a passionate seeker of truth on a quest for personal and neurological wholeness, biochemical balance, physical health. I have found these perspectives to be immensely helpful as they have occurred to me in my work as a therapist and healer. My first and much longer book, *SIMPLIFYING THE ROAD TO WHOLENESS,* tells the back story of personal experiences in much greater detail, including the research and decades of learning that brought me to the ideas put forth more succinctly and perhaps more practically in this little book which includes my *Formula for Wholeness and Unified Theory of the Self.* Since our human condition seems to keep us from remembering the easiest things we can do for ourselves to get us out of angst, I suggest we use the numbers **1-2-3** and the letters **A-B-C** as a simple formula or guide to getting on board with what I present herein, a guide for remembering how to see and step back from the human condition and find an easier place out of which to live.

Along my own journey toward wholeness I met with several "fateful detours" and what seemed to be "wrong turnings." Carl Jung suggested that such "fateful detours and wrong turning" were part of everyone's road to wholeness. I'm not certain that any of our apparent wrong turnings or bad choices are actually mistakes in the final analysis of our lives. I am certain, however, that for most of us life does not proceed in a straight line forward, onward and upward. My own experiences of apparent detours have included medical diagnoses that were terrifying and at least one family tragedy.

As a young mother of two little children and a workaholic husband, I experienced thyroid cancer and several autoimmune diseases. Three different doctors diagnosed me with MS, and I had a positive Rheumatoid

Factor and diagnosis of Rheumatoid Arthritis and possibly Lupus. I had these challenging concerns along with thyroid cancer with much depression while I was in my 30's. I was separated from my thyroid gland, surgically, at age 30. Then, in my early 40's I shook off the other energies of illness when got divorced and moved full speed ahead with newfound health. I HAD to find wholeness as I was on my own. *I was determined to live my Soul's purpose, and that commitment filled me with the power to heal myself.* I was humming along happily and in good health but against my intuition's better judgement got remarried when I truly had wanted to keep my focus on my creative pursuits and find deeper levels of Selfhood as well as greater degrees of personality integration and wholeness. Alas, a detour into re-marriage. Another divorce and then time to create and explore all manner of new ideas emerging in science.

In the midst of my forward movement my daughter, who was a 29-year old attorney – one who had graduated with honors from Duke University and UCLA Law

School – was hit by an uninsured, reckless driver while vacationing in Maui. She lost her leg, had a C2 neck fracture, a badly broken jaw and a head injury. This was life changing for the whole family. It was not the first family trauma. Twenty three years earlier when my son, Kevin, was three years old he had been diagnosed with a life-threatening blood disease, and we were told that if he even sneezed or bumped his head he would hemorrhage internally and die. There was little hope for him except for the possibility of what the doctors called a possible "spontaneous remission". If we were to be blessed with such a spontaneous remission, we were told it would not get him out of danger for at least four months. But a merciful and miraculous instantaneous healing with my son opened me to the world of energy and Soul power. I had no background or understanding of energy work prior to my son's illness and miraculous healing. Details of this healing miracle can be found in my first book, SIMPLIFYING THE ROAD TO WHOLENESS. Kevin's miracle was a dramatic introduction into a new world of subtle yet tremendously powerful energies. With the blessed surprise of my son's healing my consciousness expanded and many adventures in healing occurred and have continued to occur. Many years later, after a good stretch of fine health, I would experience breast cancer a few years after a diagnosis of a life-threatening blood disorder. All of these ordeals offered more opportunities for growth and inner expansion.

Mine is a life of challenges overcome, much healing of both physical illness and significant depressions. Sexual abuse at age three and complexity going back generations were all part of the mix. Grief and gratitude, tragedy and triumph have given me the opportunity to uplift others out of my life experiences.

I have noticed how the energies of life seem to compensate, balance each other. Joy has been present at the Ground of my Being as I feel it is found within each of us. Often I have lost touch with that essential energy of aliveness before I employed the "formula" put forth herein. I believe that liberation and healing abounds for those of us who seek wholeness with passion. This has been my experience and the experience of many clients. In fact, I believe, this wholeness already exists within us and it holds us, although we may not be conscious enough of the energy – the best dimension of us – that is holding the rest of us. That best dimension of who we are can be found, felt and reclaimed throughout our lives. We seem to move in and out of the consciousness that feels like freedom from suffering when we are experiencing the richest level of our Being. Too often we allow life and a variety of personality patterns to distract us from what matters most – our Essence. Our very precious Essence!

My creative imagination and openness to spiritual inspiration has given me new theories and perspectives and a synthesis of many modalities I've learned during my studies. I've had a sizable urge to share them. Please read on. And do not be annoyed with the redundancy, the oft-repeated comments. Such repetition is designed to have an almost hypnotic affect so the basic simple concepts herein find a home in the reader's unconscious mind.

CHAPTER TWO

Setting The Stage for 1-2-3

Arriving at the perspectives put forth in this book has been both a linear, sequential process, and it has also been a holistic one. The linear, sequential perspective has been based on one learning experience of my life leading to the next mode of my practice, like building blocks. It has also been a non-linear process with sudden flashes of seeing the whole of things, holistic. A synthesis has appeared. I have a fun habit of listening to my inner Whole Brain Advisor, which was the name of a "Dear Abby" type Q and A column I wrote years ago for Conscious Choice, a Chicago area magazine. I like to consider a "right-brain" answer, metaphorically speaking, as well as a "left-brain" response to puzzles, problems, or questions that come my way.

Profound self-help can happen with the *Human Growth Process*^{TM} introduced and put forth in the last chapter of this book. Remembering certain basics can be challenging in our busy lives. Perhaps we can help ourselves get to a peaceful place of authentic wholeness if we can simply remember to count to three with awareness of the meaning of these numbers used in a helpful context. Simply remember **A-B-C**. The formula is: **1-2-3**, **A-B-C**. More about this easily-remembered formula shortly.

Humanness is a complicated condition. It often seems like the human condition is too hard, too much of a struggle. There is very little about living out of our human condition that is easy; to be a person in a chaotic world is difficult. May this book make the process of our growth occur with greater degrees of grace. May the reader, self-helper or counselor alike, find faster access to the place within each of *us beyond the human condition*, where peace resides. Peace and joy.

A great many techniques have emerged in the field of psychology since the good Doctor Freud uncovered the unconscious mind and gave birth to the field of psychology. As a well-trained and immensely curious psychotherapist, I have consumed dozens of post-graduate training programs in the multitude of approaches that have emerged during my decades of practicing psychotherapy. In no way do I wish to discount the techniques and helpful approaches to the human condition which abound these days. Indeed, many of the techniques have been helpful, and I continue to use a mixture of many of the systems of psychotherapy which I have learned from many branches of the field of counseling, healing, and psychotherapy. However, sometimes while exploring and often mastering the vast array of techniques therapists use and reading the overwhelming number of books – self-help and text books and journals – *the essentials can get lost.* The essentials of who we are first and foremost! It is our Essence that needs to be kept in view as our primary identity and goal. Readers of this little book who are seeking personal growth and well-being may find relief herein. And therapists reading these pages can make the healing and growth of our clients and ourselves less frustrating than it sometimes is. We can make it less complicated by presenting a formula and awareness of a growth process for living life which simplifies, helps us to remember and keeps us attending to basics. Could it be that the basics are all we really need? Often, this is the case.

Just as an adolescent seeks his or her identity as an important stage of psychological development, we as adults are continually seeking to experience our wholeness, our Unified Soul Self. And we may continually move toward a more cohesive personality self. We may be doing this seeking unconsciously. Hopefully we are more often *consciously* longing for and seeking this growth into wholeness. The power of our intentions cannot be underestimated.

The numbers one, two and three in this holistic Human Growth Process*TM* represent a three-in-one look at reality. Three different ways to observe and experience reality. Different from each other, One, Two and Three are all true. Three perspectives on how we are experiencing ourselves at a particular time. It is easy to remember **1-2-3** as you move forward and read on. **A-B-C** will follow.

It is liberating to awaken to where we are standing, to know which stance we are operating out of, and to flow from one realm to another with a high degree of consciousness. Living in this way becomes a dance, a dance with three stances (and even four).

As I've been amused when my clients have called me their "shrink" when I've thought of myself as the very opposite of a head-shrinker, we can each think of ourselves as finding the arena of "expanded consciousness". The simple formula, 1-2-3, A-B-C can do this for us. I hope my clients have been amused when they ask me for their diagnosis and I respond, "You have too much of the human condition," for that is what the problem is. Too much interference from our physical, mental and emotional body when our true Essence longs to be in the foreground of our life. Once our Essence or ONEness realm takes its rightful position of sovereignty in the scheme of things even our biochemistry can move toward balance.

CHAPTER THREE

One is for Essence

ONE represents a pre-existing condition of *wholeness.* Every individual has this pre-existing condition of wholeness, no matter how unbalanced he or she may seem to be at the level of physical and/or psychological self. Remembering this and frequently reminding ourselves of this underlying condition of wholeness needs to be foremost in our thoughts about ourselves. Life is easier as we hold this as our *primary identity.* It is the single most important thing for us to remember in this holistic Human Growth Process *TM*. Once we have the habit of remembering that this essential condition of wholeness is who we are, once we keep this perspective in the foreground of our perceptions of ourselves, life can flow along with considerably less angst.

Simply put, we have two modes: Our Wholeness which we can think of as our Greater Condition, AND then we have our Human Condition out of which our challenges are experienced. Ultimately, it is all good but it simplifies our experience of living to notice, frequently, which dimension is dominant at a particular time.

ONE represents our condition of the wholeness of our very being, our soul, which embraces and holds all our potentials and all that we have and will experience in our frequently fragmented human condition. This condition of our Oneness, essentially our Greater Condition which reflects the Creative Forces and allows us to feel at one with everything, is in contrast to our human condition. It is our human nature which is what the focus is all about in the fields of psychology and psychiatry. The human condition, our psychological realm, is intimately related to our physical, neurological, biochemical nature. Our emotions impact often dramatically on our human condition. In fact, every thought impacts immediately on our biology, often creating uncomfortable imbalances. We can live far more comfortably if we keep our Oneness or Wholeness dimension in the primary position of our identities. Our human condition is best seen as secondary. Alas, we humans spent most of our life swimming around in our humanness, occasionally almost drowning in it.

Quite apart from this physical human condition we have our essential BEING, our **ONE**ness. We can call it our Creative Condition, Our Greater Self. The condition that reflects Divinity, Our Soul. Even for those who may not relate to the notion of a soul, one can simply consider it as the totality of all that we are, have been and can be. I suspect that at a deep level we all seek "soulful functionality", something a client once told me he was seeking. It is the larger dimension of our consciousness that embraces without judgment all that we are, physical and non-physical. That would be the wholeness, or Soulness. The energy of our ONEness or Soul realm is without judgment and, when we are aligned with this domain we feel the wind at our back, gently moving us forward with our Soul's purpose, lovingly filling us with a feeling of "let's get on with it." *We never feel stuck when we are in our **ONE**ness dimension.* It is the perspective of an all-embracing inclusiveness. The following image may help bring this sense of our own wholeness into focus. It is our Great Self that holds, embraces our human condition in all its complexity. We can call our humanness our Little Self, fascinating and talented as it might be. It is, after all, mortal. Fortunately we ARE something more. We have a Great Self and we HAVE, for a limited stay, our psychological, physical Little Self which longs for cohesiveness. Life is infinitely more manageable when we put our Oneness, our Great Self in the position of sovereignty.

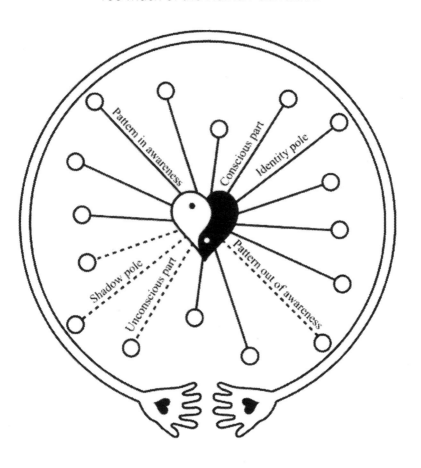

ONE also represents, to me, The Holy Whole, The Grand Container of All That Is, the Creative Forces whose image we reflect. When we identify, first and foremost with this Essence or our Soul, all wounds and alleged pathology pale by comparison. Consider for a moment the whole of your life up until now. We may think of the whole of our life experience as "the good, the bad and the ugly," as it is frequently described. When we deal with parts of our human condition, life feels out of balance. Now imagine that you are backing up, glancing at your whole life through the largest possible picture frame and holding it in your consciousness, in your awareness. A sense of balance more often than not occurs when we do this. Somehow, for most, life experiences seem to compensate for one another. Integration of our often fragmented human condition or personality happens much more rapidly when we remember and help others remember that they are *primarily* a wholeness/soulness – a **ONE**ness. As individuals we simply feel better as we keep this perspective in our vision. If we are in the helping professions or in a healing role, we notice that as clients reflect on the totality of their lives from this vantage point, they frequently perceive that a balance of pleasure and pain has been experienced. As I have observed the lives of hundreds of clients, life seems to be *compensatory* for those who seek the expansion of consciousness. Those with particularly painful early lives find happiness of a commensurate degree in later life which balances the previous pain, *if* they choose to awaken to the unity of their soul. Difficulties can more easily be accepted simply as "aspects" of one's totality when we look at our life through this largest possible picture frame, through the eyes of the soul.

Ralph Waldo Emerson, always an inspirational voice for me, frequently wrote about the compensatory nature of life, how aspects of our life experience are balanced by opposite experiences.

I described the perspective of **ONE**ness, wholeness, to a 30 year old client who was over-identified with her wounds and symptoms. Her parents had divorced; she had a very disturbed mother and an alcoholic father, certainly reasons for complexity and concern. During our second session I shared my cosmology with her. Although highly intelligent and educated, this woman had no world view which could serve her growth. One of the first things I noticed 35 years ago when I embarked on a holistic way of practicing was that many clients had no way of thinking about life in general, or their own lives in particular, from which they could get to any place that was more comfortable. Many had no world view out of which to live a more manageable life. Like many people, my client had simply sought symptom relief. This was what my academic and professional training had taught me to provide but it did not seem sufficient; I wanted to share with clients a way of comprehending reality, inner and outer reality. During our second session I shared with her a perspective of the psychological self of our human nature AND ALSO helped her access the easier place out of which to live, the Soul/Greater, Larger Self.

That night this client dreamt about exploring a twelve million dollar house and noticed a cracked tile in one of the bathrooms; she then continued through the house. After this dream's message was understood the client needed very few sessions as she shifted into identifying with her wholeness. Our soul is indeed a mansion, a castle containing our wounds, mere cracked tiles to simply notice, experience energetically and accept and move beyond. In one of her major works, *The Interior Castle,* (1577) Theresa of Avila wrote of the soul as a beautiful mansion in which God resides in the centermost place. One can consider one's own heart as a reflection of divinity. Healing happens once we get the spacious picture. I've put it poetically:

Oh spacious soul,

My grand container

Which heals and holds this life's sum total,

You nurture possibilities within —

As waves you flow

Beyond the fleshy boundaries of my skin.

You fold, within your arms, my personality.

You hold and yet you set me free.

For as I'm conscious of YOUR energy

I AM expanded, grandly

Connecting, then, with ONE and all

And listening, may hear "the call."

(N. Ging, 2000)

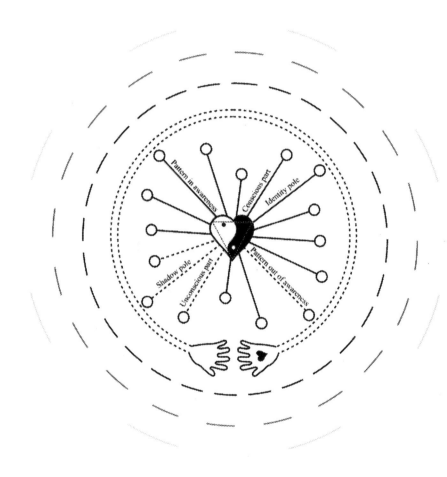

We can recognize that we are in the mode of **One**ness by the sense of wonder, peace, completeness, safety, fullness and trust which we feel in our physical body. *ONE*derful, *WONDER*ful, **One**derFULL, **ONE**ness. The sense of balance and integration is actually palpable.

AN EXERCISE: Simply ask yourself to recall a feeling of thorough well-being. Perhaps thinking of a moment or accomplishment or achievement, or perhaps being in a most beautiful, safe place in Nature. If no such memory emerges, make one up.

Most, but not all, can remember at least a moment when a feeling occurred that matched the words of William Wordsworth, "All's right with the world" even when we remember that there are many difficult aspects of our own life and far too much chaos in the world at large. The words of William Wordsworth convey the experience of **ONE**ness. This simple exercise is healing to the nervous system. It is practical from a neuropsychology perspective to let ourselves remember a time when we felt a sense of joy, delight, accomplishment. *Buddha's Brain; A Practical Neuroscience of Happiness, Love and Wisdom* by Rick Hanson, Ph.D., and Richard Mendius, M.D., are a good resource for more details about this process. There is a particular quality of relaxation to this perspective which one can learn to recognize and physically feel. This unity consciousness of the stance of **ONE** reflects "All That Is." Yet it is not the *only* stance there is. The human condition carries with it a vast capacity for experiencing life in **TWOs.**

CHAPTER FOUR

Two is for Two Realities

TWO represents two things:

1. **TWO** represents *two* different modes or interpretations of reality, **AND IT ALSO**
2. represents personality duos or pairs of opposite energies balancing each other as polarities. Energetic polarities.

Mythologist Joseph Campbell (1989) said, "The world is divided into two kinds of people; those who see the world in twos and those who don't." With this I doubly agree.

It appears that we are hard-wired to experience life in two qualitatively different realities. The often painful work of life on earth is more manageable as we learn to dance between these **two** realities with growing awareness of the choice to raise or lower the volume on one dimension or the other, or to notice which reality is in the foreground and which is in the background in any particular moment.

Exercise: *Developing a habit of paying attention to which reality has dominance at any one time can yield great rewards in the form of expanded levels of consciousness.* **Bringing ourselves to such awareness intermittently is a practice worth embracing.**

Seeking balance with the **two** dimensions, the **two** realities brings us greater health and well-being. Just as there are the natural polarities of the created world – night/day, dark/light, Earth/Heaven, female/male – there are also **two** qualitatively different realities for which a separate set of "laws" seem, to me, to apply. It is my sense that our brains are equipped to interpret reality in two major ways. Moving into this perspective of double vision, getting to know and value the rules of each reality makes the rigors of living easier. It also enlarges and ennobles us.

The following Table gives an overview to the two different realities. There is a spectrum of energy from dense to spacious. To get a feeling for the two different realities in their most polarized state, they are described in the Table below.

The Energy Paradigm	The West's 'Real World' Paradigm
Reality as waves of interconnected energy	Reality as particles (separate parts)
Energy in motion	More dense fixed patterns
Reality as Quantum Physics knows it to be	Reality as Particle (Newtonian) Physics
Focus is on the Whole	Focus is on the Parts
Spaciousness. Mostly empty space.	Particles coalescing into form, structure
Spiritual	Material: Physical-Mental-Emotional
Vague, amorphous, abstract, random	Concrete and much more easily measured

Invisible	Visible
Known through intuition or 6th (vibrational) sense	Known through 5 physical senses
Mysterious	Understandable - understood
Power of a mysterious kind - awe inspiring power.	Power of a more concrete and measurable kind
Honors the mystery World of imagination is boundless	Seeks mastery of human life and nature World of material reality has limits
"Implicate order" "Enfolded"	"Explicate order" "Unfolded"
David Bohn Quote: "There are no nouns ….	…. only slow verbs."
The spaces between the notes	The notes themselves
The spaces between the in-breath and out-breath	The action of breathing the in and out breaths

Infinite	Finite
Oneness "All are One"	Separateness, differentiation. We are separate individuals who can be maturely interdependent
We're all in this together.	Lily Tomlin: "We're all in this alone."
Concerned with being	Concerned with doing
Imagination	Information
Primary Process	Secondary Process
Unknown to the ego (Primary Process) Known through soul consciousness	Experienced mostly with the ego (Secondary Process)
Spirituality as Seeking experience of ALIVENESS A whole-body experience	Spirituality Looking for MEANING in life, a more mental phenomenon

Our personal, internal world reflects these two realities.

As it is in the world outside of us, so it is within ourselves; there are **TWO** qualitatively different dimensions of our personhood. Primarily we ARE a large Self (our spacious, gracious soul, our wholeness) and secondarily, we HAVE a little self (our human nature, personality, physical body). This simple perspective alone, at its most basic level, is helpful as we consider it. Curious minds may want to know more so I will elaborate.

In 1989 a thought occurred to me which felt like a joyful "mindgasm." My "Ah HA!" was this: what is referred to as "Right brain thinking," or the feminine (Yin) principle, seems to interpret reality in the way that Quantum Physics describes reality. On the other hand, "left brain thinking," the male (Yang) principle, interprets reality as described by the scientific paradigm of the western world since the seventeenth-century, Newtonian Physics. My particularly pleasurable intuitive flash came after many years of study and questioning. (Intuition seems to work best when it is "informed intuition," when we have accrued some information or knowledge about the areas into which we are asking our soul to dip, beseeching the Creative Forces and bring us answers). This questioning began for me when I was a toddler, and it has never stopped. The "How and Why" series of books were my favorite in my childhood. As I have reviewed my life, those moments in which I felt the most joy and passion, the most aliveness, were those times when I felt I was participating in the creation of a bridge between science and spirituality. Perhaps it is true for everyone that when we are being most true to our own particular soul's purpose we feel a certain quality of aliveness. It may be useful to review one's life looking for those moments when such energy of particular aliveness was felt. This can be a clue to our soul's purpose.

(Note: I have a strong hunch that our own particular Soul will not let us release our body, make our transition or die, until we have fulfilled our Soul's purpose. Stephen

Hawking was given a diagnosis of ALS a quarter of a century ago. His moral life was extended defying all expectations. Could it be that his Soul knows he had additional important things to contribute to Science?) For those whose lives appear to be cut short at a young age, perhaps their Soul's purpose was accomplished by the lives they touched. There will always be room for mystery in this area.)

Several steps and stages over many years were building blocks for my curiosity, preparing me to be receptive to new insights. The first such moment came in the early 1960 when I heard O. Hobart Mower speak about his book *The Crisis in Psychiatry and Religion*. I was a young undergraduate at Michigan State University. His topic stimulated a dimension of me (at that time did not consciously realize it was my Soul) to such a degree that I felt as if a jolt of electricity had gone through me, and I felt "the call" deep within my body sense. The relationship between science and spirituality confounded me; these two areas of study and experience became my constant companions from that time on. In the early 1970's I found myself fascinated with the emerging perspective of "right brain and left brain" cognition. I was also impressed with and personally aided by the work of psychoanalyst Heinz Kohut, creator of Self Psychology which was fun as I always enjoy the mental masturbation of a good theory, but psychoanalysis actually has little to do with the ideas herein. Here I would add, sadly, that analytic psychotherapy can actually keep people stuck in their evaluative, analytical mind, away from heartfully knowing, truly experiencing their wholeness. It has been said that "analysis is paralysis". Yet Kohut's work spoke to me in a particular way as he taught of an arch that bridged a particular set of energies within the personality: grandiosity and idealization, a bridging of polarities. This is something that has always rung true for me.

By the late 1970's I was learning about The New Sciences. Quantum Physics particularly intrigued me because the way in which this New Physics viewed reality was much like the perspective held by the many metaphysical teachers I had been meeting and whose psychic structures I was researching. Personally I was experiencing thyroid cancer, depression, serious autoimmune and neurological diseases which added urgency to my quest for a perspective that could bring me to health, wholeness. I noted that spiritual healers and psychics (and other such triple P's: Primary Process People) had certain personality, relationship and cognitive proclivities. One of their peculiarities was seeing the world as "energy in motion." Quantum Physics also describes a world of waves of energy in motion; one of its architects, David Bohm said, "There are no nouns, only slow verbs." In other words, there are no concrete separate objects with molecular form; rather everything is in process: "This isn't paper, it is papering," he would say.

The paradigm of conventional science fathered by Isaac Newton is known as "Particle Physics." It describes a world made up of separate particles, things with molecular form, boundaries. Modern science is based on Newtonian Physics, but this perspective or science, it seems, is only half the story. It has been and will continue to be a useful paradigm for many aspects of life, but it is not sufficient for where humanity is going. The workings of subtle energies and spiritual experience cannot be explained or well-studied out of this paradigm of Particle Physics. Reportedly, 70% to 90% of all people have numinous, supernatural, "woo-woo" experiences which cannot be explained or even described in terms of the conventional scientific paradigm. The paradigm of Quantum Mechanics helps. Yet those who write about Quantum healing and the vision that "all is one" aren't presenting the most practical perspective for psychological differentiation, for moving into (little) selfhood, or our personality individuation. In the larger, all-embracing reality, everything seems to be interconnected waves of energy and we are all one interconnected family of humanity. On another level, in the reality of form, molecular structure, of which Particle

Physics teaches, we are separate individuals. In one reality "we are all in this together." In another reality, "We are all in this (pausing) alone," said Lily Tomlin as a bag-lady in "The Search for Signs of Intelligent Life in the Universe." Both perspectives are true. Developing a kind of "double vision" with our two different dimensions, or helping our clients do this if we are therapists, can create balance, health. I propose yet another paradigm which is a marriage between the Reality of a ONENESS perspective *with* the Reality of SEPARATENESS, not a merger but a mutually respectful partnership.

The words "spirituality" and "religion" reflect the two different realities. Spirituality is the *esoteric* level of religious or non-religious traditions and of the Quantum/feminine principle. By contrast, religion at the *exoteric* level, has form and structure, is of the Yang mode, known in an identifiable, particle/molecular way.

The experience of our self without a separate, individual identity does not for a functional, healthy human make, yet some spiritual teachers would encourage this **ONE**ness perspective as all that matters. Stressing our **ONE**ness without also being aware of the dualistic nature of our human brains can create fears of merging and losing one's individual identity. As clinicians we need to teach our clients about differentiating themselves from their families of origin. Psychotherapy supports the work of individuated selfhood. I tell most clients the story of separation-individuation and the all good versus all bad (i.e., the pleasure of having one's needs met versus the pain of hunger, etc.) perspective of our first few years of life. This split is ideally resolved into healthy psychological self-hood as a child and teen matures. This is a linear, sequential, developmental, male mode, "left-brain" perspective. This is psychological work. It is my belief that we best serve our clients by presenting them with the reality of separateness, while *also* experiencing with them the perspective of the other paradigm, the energy paradigm, in which we are all one unity of intermingling waves of energies. Healers and clinicians doing "energy work" generally work out of the perspective of Quantum Physics. Academically trained clinicians are educated out of the conventional Newtonian paradigm of Western Science. We can honor both realms, demonstrating to our clients how to dance between and respect these two realities.

What we have seen as pathology or immaturity may sometimes be an issue of mixing paradigms. Magical thinking is not always a sign of mental illness or developmental arrest; this child-like magical thinking way of comprehending reality is reflective of the energy paradigm. In the physical, material world vampires only rarely exist and suck blood. However, "energy vampires" do exist in great numbers, sucking subtle energies from others; they can be a dangerous drain to our well-being. The notion of vampires reflects the energy paradigm but are depicted in terms of the conventional and more concrete paradigm. Another example of mixing paradigms is this: "Step on a crack, you break your mother's back," is merely a simple rhyme of childhood, at least in the 1940's when I heard it. The message of that rhyme is impossible in the conventional paradigm of reality. Yet it may reflect a child's affinity for the reality that all things are interconnected and we can affect each other energetically with our thought waves, as well as our actions. We are speaking truth in terms of the energy paradigm when we say that an infant comes "straight from Heaven." The paradigm of The Whole, The One Interconnectedness of ALL is the energy paradigm and the world of "Primary Process", or unconscious knowing. An infant emerges into physical earthly experience already equipped with energy sensitive, intuitive, random, impressionistic, sensual ways of knowing. Modern psychology has taught us that primary process experience which dominates in the first five or six years of life is to be replaced by secondary process experience as the "age of reason" emerges and the ego develops. Rather than being *replaced by* secondary process, primary process need to be *balanced with* secondary process. The form and structure of secondary process makes life more predictable and manageable. We have been taught about the human condition in a developmental, sequential, linear, secondary process way, which is only half the story. There is an additional way of comprehending and interpreting the experience of living.

Remarkable healing can occur when we bring the two modes of reality into relationship with one another. For example, a client came to my office for pre-surgical hypnosis for a liver transplant which she was scheduled to have the following week. She had a life-threatening liver disease and was told that surgery could not be put off any longer. At the time of her liver diagnosis, this client was the age her mother was when her mother died. For this reason, my client had asked her doctors to postpone the surgery until she had her next birthday, getting her past an ominous chronological age for her. During the months of waiting she had several additional tests to check on the condition of her liver. That organ was in a very serious state of ill-health.

The time had finally come for surgery. She had told me of her Christian background which had been a positive orientation for her. Fortunately, heavy emotional baggage of guilt from an oppressive version of Christianity had not been her experience. Her healthy Christian background connoted only love. My usual protocol includes asking a client to visualize anyone who represents unconditional healing love placing their hands over the area where there is an energy blockage, pain or disease. Because of her positive feelings about Jesus since her childhood, I suggested that she visualize Jesus' hands over her liver and I asked her to speak to her liver, thanking it for its years of service, saying good-bye to it. (This might sound ridiculous before one realizes the aliveness and consciousness of every organ, every cell). "Tell your liver to be a love sponge," I continued. Using a series of pre-surgical hypnotic suggestions, I prepared her body to cooperate with the surgery. One of the suggestions given before surgery is that there will be very little bleeding during surgery. I am always amazed when clients tell me after their surgery that the doctor reported that there had been very little bleeding, for there is a skeptical part of me that doesn't entirely believe these hypnotic suggestions can work!

As I relaxed more deeply along with my client, I asked her to imagine the image of the sacred heart of Jesus, with fire's flames flickering out of the heart; I suggested she see this sacred-heart superimposed upon her own heart. We then both visualized and intended for the healing Light of the heart to fill her liver, while at the same time I had her do eye movement as I had been trained to do with the EMDR (Eye Movement and Desensitization and Reprocessing) technique.

At the end of the session, as she was leaving my office, she said she could actually feel warmth flowing out of her hands into her liver. I asked her to call me as soon as she was able after the liver transplant. Two days after our session she called with her news: She had gone into the surgical suite, then went under anesthesia. When she awoke she was told by her surgeon that they did the often repeated liver scope which she had had many times in the previous years all showing a very sick liver. This time, in the operating room ready to perform a liver transplant the doctors had discovered with the scoping procedure that she no longer needed the liver transplant! A rather miraculous happening (documented at University of Illinois Medical Center) and one we did not expect. But *the reality of the more dense physical body encountered the reality of the higher vibrations, invited by the Soul's spacious consciousness.* I'm convinced that miracles often occur by bringing the Light of the higher vibrations into areas of ill health in our dense physical body.

Finding health, which means essentially finding our balance, becomes much easier as we become attuned to **TWO** realities. Sometimes chaotic brain chemistry requires bio-chemical help – anti-depressants or anti-anxiety drugs – or we can seek improvement for faulty wiring in neurological structures with eye movement therapies, sound and light treatments, etc. These days, help abounds for people with small, medium or large imbalances. But when we learn to live with greater consciousness of the two realities we are experiencing, greater biochemical balance can occur without so much medical intervention.

This is not a mere exercise in abstract thinking. These realities actually have different textures and can be felt physically. In the early 1980's I took the Reiki trainings, then MariEL training with the great spiritual Soul, Ethel Lombardi. Later I learned more from the compelling world of Energy Medicine, especially from several week-long workshops with Robert Jaffee, M.D. and dozens of attunement sessions with Paul Ditscheit, M.S., and several five-day intensive workshops with Donna Eden and treatments with Dr. Sara Allen. I have learned to feel and teach clients to feel the difference between the dense emotional and physical energies and the qualitatively different, more subtle energies of consciousness.

The beauty of the Holistic Growth Process which I'm delighted to present here is that we are able to bring about much transformation for ourselves. The very energy of Consciousness, our primary reality, directed into our secondary reality of the human condition, i.e., the more dense energy of emotions or even physical pain, *actually transforms*. We can learn to live as *transformers* of our own energies. We can *transcend the human condition* when we want to get out of emotional discomfort. Transformation occurs in a remarkable meeting – when and where the two qualitatively different realities, found on opposite ends of a spectrum of energy, meet the other. The dense energy of our human condition, our secondary realm, can be infused with the power of the spaciousness of our primary reality, our Soul's Essence.

While much of life, like light, is both wave and particle, it is helpful when we consider our life experiences in **TWO** different ways: 1) those which are of a sixth-sense, subtle-energy nature and 2) those which are comprised of more coarse or dense vibrational textures and experiences with our five more earthy physical senses. Once someone has experienced the physical feeling of the more subtle Soul's energy, a newfound feeling of unconditional self-love emerges. Unconditional love is not to be equated with self-esteem for the latter is so often conditional, based on our accomplishments. The personality realm benefits from self-esteem, of course, but there is a more powerful experience of unconditional acceptance that emerges out of the primary realm of Essence. This experience of self-love from the larger, Greater Self or Higher Astral Plane of Soul, and is felt in the heart, we can look at and accept more of the human ways of the small self of personality.

The Soul energy not only holds or contains the learnings from the emotions, thoughts, and sensations of the body, it also infuses them with life force, or energy. Both our Soul and our human nature are divinely energized in this process. The philosophy of Pantheism holds that everything in nature is filled with divine life force. Another philosophy, Panantheism presumes that "Something" *holds* all aspects of nature which are filled with divine life force. The perspective I am presenting, therefore, could be considered to be Panantheistic. A force holds all that is just as our Soul holds all our humanness. As above, so below.

CHAPTER FIVE

Another Two—Our Internal Duos

The Other Duo of TWO

In addition to the **TWO** realities, and therefore **TWO** ways of experiencing ourselves within those **TWO** different perceptions, another level of **TWO**'s exists. These are the pairs of opposites with our personality. All have experienced the paradoxes of human existence, often confounding. If we draw a diagram or demonstrate a visual image of the "arms" of the Soul's wholeness embracing, encircling the complexity of one's more concrete life experiences of the biological, human level, one is able to open to greater awareness of his/her many personality polarities. Like light and shadow, or two sides of a single coin, there are two sides of our many personality patterns. Looking at this in an ideal way, we can grow to know and hold both sides in awareness with an equal degree of awe and reverence.

One example: Many professional caretakers will recognize within themselves a nurturing, care-taker pattern *balanced by* a needy inner child pattern, a part of oneself which may sometimes be outside of awareness and projected onto others. Another polarity might be feeling superior to others on one hand and feeling inferior to other people at other times. Perhaps one might notice a pattern of feeling "not good enough" being compensated for, or balanced by another energy of equal intensity such as arrogance, perfectionism, etc. We all contain many paradoxes. Being human can be arduous, to put it politely. This human condition may become more comfortable as we look at these paradoxes in a new way.

Splitting is the psychological term for being in touch with one side of the coin while losing touch with the other side of the personality. This can sometimes be intense polarization of personality patterns. This polarization need not be seen or experienced as pathology or even immaturity. People displaying "ego-splitting" commonly called a "split personality" can be viewed as having what I like to think of as *too much of the human condition*. Or not enough awareness of the Soul's **ONE**ness reality. Lack of awareness of the Soul's wholeness creates what at times can be extreme behavior on the part of polarities within the personality realm.

Polarities are actual energetic realities. Newton's law teaches that for every action there is an equal and opposite reaction. The Book of Ecclesiastes, 3:1-8, tells of fourteen pairs of behavioral opposites – "a time to speak and a time to remain silent," etc. – concluding with the comforting phrase "….and a time for every purpose under Heaven." Acceptance of "all that is" represents psychological cohesiveness, "having it together" and also wholesome spirituality. Swiss psychiatrist, Carl Jung, essentially taught that for everything that is true the opposite is also true.

Daniel Levinson's Yale University research (1978) on adult development presented four polarities which all adults much face: Dependent-Independent, Young-Old, Male-Female, Creative-Destructive.

Another academician who enjoyed a good theory, psychoanalyst Heinz Kohut mentioned earlier, created an entire theory of narcissism as he addressed simply one "narcissistic" polarity. He saw this as grandiosity at one pole and idealization on the other (1971).

Many polarities have their mature and immature forms. There often exist in an adult what can be noted as primitive polarities. These are intense polarities with roots in early childhood and not at all neutralized or balanced by healthy emotional development.

EXERCISE: Take the particular polarity of the vulnerable, deeply wounded pattern within, and imagine experiencing the enraged child part at the other end of this energetic polarity. Visualize the enraged part on one end of a see-saw and picture the deeply hurt part on the other. Ask these opposite primitive patterns or parts to look in each other's

eyes and exchange a little energy with each other. As a result the enraged pattern becomes softer and the hurt pattern becomes stronger, less vulnerable. Meanwhile the neutral awareness of Soul energy is lending its profound healing energy to the process by simply being a witness to what is occurring between the pair of personality energies. Simply holding the duo on the see-saw, breathing and letting the energies seek a more balanced place.

$\mathscr{P}$olarities Sharing a See-Saw

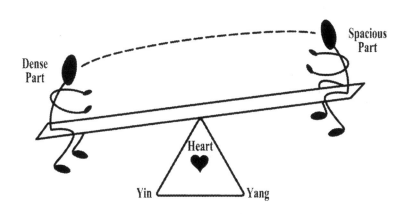

EXERCISE: When noticing an uncomfortable feeling or mind-set, focus on it intently while realizing that

every aspect of our human condition has an equal and opposite energy pattern. Ask that the opposite pattern be brought to the surface so you can put those two opposite ends of a polarity on the see-saw. Breathe deeply, remembering that your heart is the fulcrum point and the Soul energy flows through the heart.

Beyond the comfortable co-existence that the partnered energies achieve through this awareness, something new may be born out of this union of opposites. For example, the energy of optimism may meet the energy of pessimism and, at the place of their encounter, the energy of hope may arise.

Seeing sub-personalities or "parts" within oneself is a perspective I first learned of in 1981 from the work of Freud's student, Roberto Assagioli (1973). In the early 90's Hal Stone's (1985) Voice Dialogue technique was useful to me as was a time when I taught at the I.F.S. Conferences and contributed an energetic perspective to the Internal Family Systems model of Richard Schwartz. "Parts work" can be useful but too much focus on looking for our "parts" can keep us in our heads with analysis. Therefore my preference is to work with "parts" as bodily felt "energies." I do not see the personality as a group of "parts" as much as energetic patterns, always in polarity, pairs seeking partnership with one another. It is then always important to return to our **ONE**ness stance, our essence, putting that in the foreground.

Polarities which we think of as neutral occur in nature. Ancient Chinese Medicine is an entire system focused around elements and energies of nature which seek to find balance. Probably all energies within the Earth and the Heavens are neutral or balance one another. However, our human nature adds a challenging twist to energies and therefore to personal polarities. This is the challenge: From our human condition's judgmental vantage point, polarities can look "good" at one end of the pole and "bad" at the other. Severely wounded individuals may fear that the "bad" will contaminate the "good" and such people may initially resist having the poles at the opposite ends of an intense polarity come into relationship with one another, until they grow accustomed to remembering who and what they are. Who and what we all are, first and foremost, is a balanced, whole Soul. We already HAVE that. We already ARE that Soul.

Most of us readily enjoy observing polarities within ourselves and in the world at large. The capacity for awareness is enhanced in the process of looking for these duos within ourselves. Practice simply noticing without judgment. This alone is profoundly healing; it allowing us to experience balance. Health and balance can be found and physically felt in an individual when the pairs of poles meet as mutually respectful partners who need each other for a sense of completeness and harmony, partnership. As more people experience the benefit of getting to know and accept their inner world's polarities and have their polarities meet for the greatest health, in the middle, there may one day be a desire for the outer world's family to have our extremely wealthy and our extremely impoverished sisters and brothers come together and share their resources, balancing economic energies with each other. Polarities don't disappear into each other, but they become less extreme as they come into a relationship with one another. Economic justice within the world may be the delusion of a social worker such as I, but it is one in which we might all wish to engage thereby creating a stronger energetic thought field out of which the physical reality of economic balance can emerge.

A & E: Awareness and Experience

Mystics have often admonished us to stay in the reality above duality. Yet what may be more realistic than staying in the higher realm is living from both 1) *awareness* of the realm of unity consciousness, or **ONE**ness and 2) the *experience* of our humanity, our human nature with its **TWO**ness, many pairs of opposite energies.

In the realm of duality where the energies of our human nature exist on a spectrum of various degrees of density and spaciousness, we *experience* our human condition, feeling the energies of our personality within our body. We frequently flow back and forth between the **TWO** realities experiencing at one moment the realm of unity consciousness and, soon thereafter, experiencing the very human realm of duality. Shifting from the more energetically spacious *AWARENESS OF* experience to the more dense energies of the emotional, physical embodied *EXPERIENCE* itself leads to moments of enlightenment! It is as easy to remember **A & E** as **1-2-3**.

Many hyper-spiritual, or "triple P" Primary Process People, use spirituality as a defense, an escape from their human condition which may be rejected as too painful when the polarities have not yet been seen, felt and embraced. Meeting such energetically sensitive individuals in their preferred realm of the vibrational

milieu, or energy paradigm, may be suitable for some –
with dream work, trance work, energy healing, art and
music therapy and the new (and ancient) potions and
notions of vibrational medicine such which are now
becoming plentiful as more of the population discovers
alternative medicine. Healing with sound vibrations,
light and even color are of profound value. However,
I'd consider balancing the paradigms by taking a
more linear, cognitive approach with highly sensitive
people. A person who is "loosey-goosey, spaced-out" or
dissociated may not need to dip into the unconscious.
An open-eyed, grounded, structured approach would
serve to bring balance and strengthen the personality
level of personhood. Conversely, a less creative, tightly
organized, over-functioning, "left brain" person could
benefit from therapies reflecting the energy paradigm
which would expand their consciousness and sense of
their large Self, the Soul Self.

If we flow back and forth between BOTH realms
yang, evaluative, linear, developmental, problem solving

realm and also *yin*, the creative, healing, vibrational, mysterious–we will get excellent guidance from our own intuition. This is especially true if we have been informed by some background in developmental psychology. The duo of **TWO**ness of informed intuition is what therapists and self-helpers can aim for. And we can easily learn which reality we need more focus upon to achieve greater balance. *Life is a balancing act* and for this the **TWO** realities of which I speak need to be honored.

EXERCISE: Here is a useful tool. Practice observing our internal energies as being on a spectrum of *energy*. A spectrum from dense to more spacious energy. Our emotions and our physical sensations are at times dense and other times more spacious. The more we put the energy of the spaciousness of our ONEness Essence realm in the foreground of our living, the more we can neutralize troublesome emotions and even lessen physical pain of our human condition.

Our work of living presents us with concrete PROBLEMS to be solved and also with MYSTERIES which are never to be solved. Existentialist Gabriel Marcel (1956) observed these two different dilemmas and wrote in an "Essay on the Ontological Mysteries," that the important things in life are mysteries and one cannot solve a mystery; one can only PARTICIPATE in a mystery. Our experience of simply BEING, or our "presence" and "participation in the mystery" of healing is the essence of the Holistic Growth Process. Mindfulness enhances our aliveness and health. A sign in my office says, "YOU MUST BE PRESENT TO WIN." Indeed, nothing in life can be lost once we learn to live from presence, from our Soul's BEINGness. In contrast, the other realm is our DOINGness. DOING the work of problem solving and strategizing around relationship issues, while still important, may become secondary, as the culture of consciousness emerges. Some say we are not *human beings* having a spiritual experience, we are *spiritual* beings having a *human* experience. Both modes are true, one in the foreground and the other in the background, depending on which paradigm we are living from or standing in at a particular moment. To be as complete as the small self of our human nature seeks to be, and to experience our large Self, connected to our spiritual sources as Spirit calls us to be, we need to recognize and feel the vibrational difference between our human experiences and our Soul's expansiveness. As with the game of golf, our stance is of profound importance. We are all best served by remembering to notice, "paradigm-wise" from whence we are coming.

Holistic techniques of the energy paradigm are often an art, a healing art. These are not as easily measured. The therapies which deal with behaviors which can be quantified or problems which can be observed and even solved are more of a science, more easily measurable. Many therapies have components of both. Therapeutic modalities might best be seen on a continuum, some being closer to the concrete, the realm of form which strengthen boundaries and improve functioning. Others therapeutic techniques, even self-help modalities, are closer to the wave-like world of the creative unconscious, where everything is connected to everything else. We are always wise to seek balance, to strive for the Aristotle's Golden Mean. With practice we can learn to notice and feel the **TWO** realities of life. As we set judgement aside, we can play with the various polarities of human experience. We can be amused by these observations. We can discover where we are coming from at a particular time, in terms of the various continuums, paradigm surfing, honoring the various aspects of the **TWO** realities of the human-divine experience.

Remember the **TWO** aspects of **TWO**:

1. pairs of polarities in the personality AND ALSO
2. two qualitatively different realms of Reality.

CHAPTER SIX

We are a Trinity

THREE: A TRINE, TRIANGLE, TRINITY

Two hemispheres and one heart

Meet to make a trinity for living;

Two perspectives of reality from mind

May find their greatest advocate in giving

Sovereignty to a heart awakened.

Once this heart-brain triangle we know

Lives will link with Grace, toward calling's

flow.

As we activate and honor this grand trine

Lives become more humane, more Divine.

(N. Ging, 2000)

The stance from which we experience our **THREE**ness
may be most important energetically. A precious triangle

in the body may be present, a potent symbol. Visualizing it can have a powerful, integrating effect. Getting to "**THREE**ness" happens as we add the particular ways of the brain's **TWO** hemispheres, or yin and yang modes, with the more Soul infused ways of the heart. As we remember the perspective of **TWO** realities and also stay aware of the personality polarities, we round out and make a triangle of this formula of remembering **1-2-3** of the holistic Human Growth Process™.

In March 2000 I attended a workshop entitled "Healing the Hardware of Your Soul" led by Daniel Amen, M.D., a neurologist and psychiatrist who said, "You cannot fulfill your soul's purpose unless your brain is working properly!" To the question, "How do I know who the real me is, if I take medication?" Amen replies, "The real you is who you are when your brain is functioning normally." Many people benefit from the wise use of medications, bringing their brain to a state of less chaos, greater normalcy, at least until traumas are worked out of the cellular memory of the body with body-centered therapy and/or the more subtle energy work with various forms of energy medicine. The bio-chemical and neurological aspects of our human condition are immensely important for the experience of psychological health. Many a client has been frustrated by an idealistic therapist saying, "Trust yourself!" People who suffer from bio-chemical imbalances or neurological deficits often realize that they cannot entirely trust their brain and/or endocrine system. Yet it must be noted that when we live more and more frequently out of the energy of our **ONE**ness, our Wholeness, our Greater Self or Soul, *then* our body often follows into that far more harmonious vibration.

One of my teacher's, Garrett Walters, has often said that the difference between someone who is mentally ill and someone who is well is the degree to which they are grounded. Grounded is the **One**ness which includes an Earthy connection while we are here, in a body. Once a physical body experiences the realm of **ONE**ness, the brain chemistry can follow into this greater harmony more easily. Once the Light Body from the spacious realm of unity or **ONE**ness infuses the dense physical body, remarkable occurrences happen.

Fortunately, in addition to the brain's wiring, there is another domain, another organ that is ever-ready to provide us with the experience of trust, courage, compassion, joy. The heart leaps out as the most precious "hardware of the soul," Daniel Amen's phrase. The heart and the brain are of two different realms, even developing separately in a very young fetus. HeartMath teaches that the heart starts beating before the brain begins to form, eventually connecting through the vagus nerve and the thalamus gland. Research on the heart-brain relationship is immensely liberating news for us all to share with one another. Heartening news!

Experiencing Sanyama Meditation on the heart in the 1980's then hearing Paul Pearsall speak on The Heart's Code at the 1998 Conference on Consciousness and Science in Albuquerque, N.M., and later visiting The Institute of HeartMath Research in 1999, taught me the effects of heart power. I have seen the growth-producing and healing effects of the heart power of individuals – electrical power out of which they can heal themselves and even help to heal those around them. The heart is more than a metaphor for healing love. It is also more than the physical organ which pumps our blood. It is, indeed, the place where we can physically experience both our Soul's realm of interconnected energies, the harmony of the "quantum" whole, compassion, acceptance and the place where our personality polarities meet in balanced personality selfhood. Cohesiveness of personality meets the power of our Soul. Within the heart we find ourselves, LARGE SELF and small self, both.

In my practice I frequently have combined energy medicine with EMDR and nearly always use body-centered psychotherapy and Psychosynthesis, "parts work", teaching clients to feel the impact of their Soul consciousness upon their more dense emotional and/or mental energies. The work of a gifted Buddhist teacher,

Reginald "Reggie" Ray, has been particularly useful in this regard. Body Centered meditation and body focused therapies are extremely important in our journey to wholeness. Body Centered meditation can bring the realms of our personhood together.

All clients I have worked with in a body-centered and/or heart-focused way, including a few diagnosed with schizophrenia, have been able to actually FEEL the experienced of the heart's realm. Most of us can truly feel that the heart is the place where past and future meet in the present moment, the eternal now, the energy of Eternity. And the heart is the place where our Soul's wholeness and the Spirit of Heaven meets Earth. It is fun to think of our body as our own personal, portable, plot of Mother Earth, for indeed we are children of the Earth as well as children reflecting the Divine aliveness of Spirit. We can re-parent ourselves as we realize and remember that the Earth is our primary Mother, and the Heavens are our Mother and Father as well.

Quickly we can move to an experience of courage and love for ourselves which emerges from our own heart. The brain will actually entrain with, or move into alignment with the heart's particular soothing and healing rhythms when one focuses on and breathes into the physical heart while remembering a time or place of harmony and gratitude.

Sweet simplicity – its bliss,

Only the heart can know this,

For bliss is not the province of the brain

Wherein complexity does reign.

Come quiet revolution,

Internal evolution,

Come heart-head marriage.

I welcome now this union

A holy whole communion.

My body is the carriage.

(N. Ging, 1999)

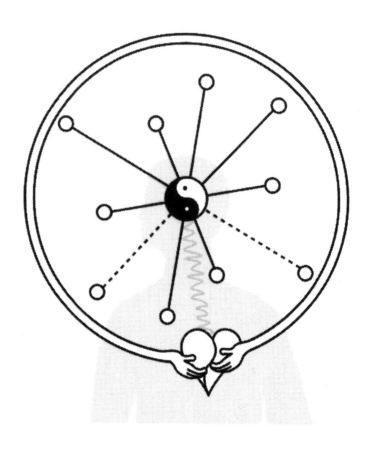

The brain, with its fear of separation and survival-based orientation, is brought to greater levels of peace when one's attention goes to the heart. Free of the survival issue the heart holds the Quantum perspective of no-separation, interconnectedness and eternal love. The heart is never confused; the brain's two hemispheres and other areas of the brain frequently experience confusion. This chaos can be abated by the particular healing electricity or vibrations of the heart. The emotions, located in the body, below the heart, are also soothed and become less extreme when one is settled in one's heart. Both the HeartMath Institute and Paul Pearsall have produced computer programs with a finger's pulse sensor which actually demonstrate the power of the heart upon the brain. According to HeartMath research, the level of an anti-aging hormone, DHEA, increases significantly when the heart's realm is moved into a leadership position. In addition, the stress hormone, Cortisol, decreases when the heart's realm is brought forth. The heart, then, must be the place where the experience of the mind's duality, polarities or **TWO**ness meet the consciousness of **ONE**ness creating a powerful trine, or triangle. Let's call it Heart-Brain Partnering. The essentials of this formula can be easy to remember as **1-2-3**.

Another aspect of **THREE** is head, heart and hara (or gut). For those not so familiar with chakras this may be helpful: The chakra system includes seven basic chakras. However the chakras are often consolidated into three areas: 1) the gut which includes first, second and third chakras, 2) the heart chakra where the lower three and upper three chakras meet, and 3) the third eye or brow chakra which includes the upper chakras.

EXERCISE: This is a beautiful and powerful meditation. Envision three violet flames, one in the gut, one in the heart and one at the forehead. Allow those three flames to burn together as one as you watch the flickering flames. Many people like to bring Saint Germain to mind whenever they think of the violet flame.

For a potentially easier time of living your life, remember **1, 2** and **3**, numbers that represent perspectives out of which we can discern our wholeness: Our **One**ness and the perspectives of our duality and our trinity. Observing ourselves with growing awareness, noticing these domains can free us from our challenging human condition. The discomfort of living from TOO MUCH OF THE HUMAN CONDITION can become a balanced condition in partnership with our Essence, our Greater Self.

In addition to **1, 2** and **3**, we can think of yet another trio: **A-B-C**. This can further assist us in our quest for wholeness.

A-B-C

The letters **A-B-C** remind us of the **A**WARE, **B**ALANCED and **C**OHESIVE personality we can create for ourselves as we attend to **1, 2** and **3**. Awakening to *awareness* of our thoughts and our emotions is what moves us toward enlightened living. Paying attention with mindful *awareness* of the polarities in our personality patterns produces a greater degree of mental and physical health. *Awareness* helps us meet the goal of feeling those polarities as the polarities find an energetic *balance* with one another.

Cohesiveness of personality is the sense of all the personality parts of which we are aware coming into relatedness, even cooperation. This cohesiveness, "having it all together", brings with it great peace.

One can add the number 4 to the simple **1-2-3** and **A-B-C** formula as we focus on the **FOUR** quadrants of the heart. I like to think that we have two yin and two yang dimensions of the heart. Some of my Energy Medicine teachers have a gift of clairvoyance; they can "see" energy. Looking at the heart chakra these gifted ones report that they "see" seven levels or layers to the heart's energy. But to keep it simple we can think of the **FOUR** chambers of the physical heart. Putting our attention on the heart awakens greater degrees of compassion and self-acceptance, *for the heart is where the most balanced energies of our human condition meet our Soul's realm.* We can imagine and trust that the heart has access to the healing energy from Heaven and Earth. We can experience profound self-acceptance when we settle into our heart and breathe in the heart's harmonious vibration of wisdom.

Developing the habit of putting one's attention on the realm of the heart and calling forth the attitude of gratitude can have surprising benefits to oneself and those around us. We seem to pump out to others harmonizing energy when we embody gratitude. Gratitude is the energetic specialty of the heart. Gratitude and harmony.

Four compartments has the heart

Housing all its qualities;

Two Yin, two Yang chambers apart

Meet Soul at their interstices.

Stout hearted, tender hearted,

Heart both Yang and Yin

Four chambered gem you are;

Soul is found within.

(N. Ging, 2000)

In summarizing, I suggest that this practical theoretical perspective, made simple by remembering **1-2-3, A-B-C**, be kept in mind in hopes of keeping in the foreground what is **most essential – our essence.**

Simply remember:

1. Who each of us is primarily: a wholeness. How one's essence or Soul experiences reality is as a **ONE**ness.

2. How our humanness experiences reality as **TWO's** – two qualitatively different realities AND also as duos, pairs of opposite patterns of emotions and thoughts. Our human condition is our physicality – mental, emotional, neurological.

3. How the awareness of our inner trine or trinity, our **THREEness**, brings our soul's unity and our dualistic, binary human nature into a trinity or triangle of Selfhood/selfhood to the healthiest degree so we can be both human and divine as we find the place where all realms meet, the heart.

Any theories or techniques of value, from either the concrete conventional medical model's paradigm or the emerging paradigm of Energy Medicine, may be used along with this **1-2-3 Formula for Human Growth** achieved holistically. Certainly, a multitude of theoretical and practical applications of psychological tools are available and helpful. However, this Formula for Wholeness keeps the essentials of our being clearly in focus as we employ whatever ever additional tools we wish to use. Perhaps nothing more than this Formula for Wholeness **1-2-3, A-B-C** will be necessary for some to feel and maintain the experience of their wholeness.

CHAPTER SEVEN

A Unified Theory of The Self ™

For those who enjoy a good theory, I offer my **Unified Theory of the Self™**; Parts and Whole, Selves and Soul which I wrote and first presented in 1992.

(Note: Most of what is contained in this chapter is integrated into the previous chapter so this will feel redundant.)

Our Soul is our wholeness – the spacious, compassionate container which holds and embraces all that we have experienced as well as our potentials. The Soul-Self is known most clearly through one's heart, the place in one's physical body where Heaven and Earth meet and where the lower three chakras meet the upper three chakras.

Our own Soul-Self is a microcosm of The Creator/God/Goddess/All That Is, The One, The Super-Conscious,

The Universe, the Macrocosm – or what I shall call The Grand Container Which Holds the Holy Whole. Just as The Grand Container "has the whole world in His/Her hands," our individual Essence/Spirit/Soul *holds* with compassionate acceptance all that we personally experience–mentally, physically, emotionally.

Within the Soul-Self there is the psychological self which CAN become cohesive when the many paradoxes, polarities or complementary pairs of opposite energy patterns of the personality are in balance and/or held with acceptance in our Consciousness, in the awareness of our Soul-Self. Energetically these pairs are as night and day, yin and yang. We may be aware of one end of the polarity while the other side or end of that polarity may be in the unconscious symbolized as the dotted lines leading to one end of the polarity.

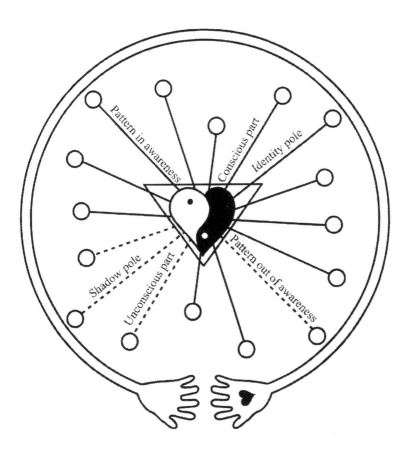

The energy of a part or pattern of personality and its opposite are equally intense as in Newtonian physics: any action has an equal and opposite reaction.

Areas of the brain operating from the male principle (linear thinking or what is popularly referred to as "left brain thinking") will experience and interpret reality as separate or concrete PARTICLES or parts. Newtonian

Physics and conventional science operates out of this paradigm. Areas of the brain functioning from the female principle ("right brain") experience and interpret reality as WAVES of intermingling energy in motion. Quantum Physics describes this realm. These realms are meant to be partners.

When the brain's dual male/female modes are functioning as a conscious partnership, we may more easily experience heart/Soul sovereignty over the often challenging human condition. Whole-hearted alignment with Heaven and Earth is achieved from the body's experience of the heart's compartments or chambers which are yin (trust, compassion tenderness, etc.) and yang (courage, joy, stout-heartedness, etc.)

The **A**ware, **B**alanced, **C**ohesive personality or psychological self is a healthy human's reflection of one's Soul-Self. The personality may be fragmented yet the Soul is always whole.

CHAPTER EIGHT

The Human Growth Process ™

Assumptions are often made about the purpose of life. Many philosophers and others who teach "The Psychology of Happiness" maintain that *the purpose of life is to be happy.*

My license plate says HEAL as I believe that many of us have to first heal enough to be able to be happy, so *the purpose of life may be primarily to heal ourselves.* Happiness follows. Ultimately, healing into a place of higher consciousness is what gives us well-being, peace and joy.

As I was enjoying my HEAL license plate, I mentioned to a man I was dating that I was looking for a car with a license plate that said GROW and I would marry that person. Kind of the glass slipper situation. Alas, the man I was dating procured the GROW license plate for his car, so how could I say "No"?

I've streamlined these steps for holistic healing in the formula put forth in earlier chapters.

What of the Human Growth Process ^{TM}? The steps involved in this process can be simplified as well as the formula presented earlier.

As I see it, The Human Growth Process ^{TM} is the Practice of Balancing Realities. In this scheme of things there are two qualitatively different dimensions of reality on either ends of the spectrum of energy. At one end of the spectrum there is the dense energy. The opposite end of that spectrum of energy is spacious, wave-like energy in motion. Those are the polarities. There is every energetic vibration in between. The balance point, where the two different dimensions of reality meet is where we can experience the best of our human nature. *There is a dimension of our Being where the best of us holds the rest of us!*

The Human Growth Process^{TM} is based on a Unified Theory of the Self. This theory can best be grasped with the visual image of the arms of the Soul embracing all the pairs of opposite parts of our human condition. Our personality, our human condition contains many paradoxes or opposite pairs of energy. These pairs can be comfortably complementary or uncomfortably polarized when we are out of balance or heavily into judgment and self-criticism. Our Soul can be seen as the compassionate, all-embracing, entirely accepting container that holds all that we are, have been and can be. This Soul of ours is beyond our mere human condition, beyond the *personality's self* which the field of psychology and psychiatry research, study and focus upon. The Soul-Self is of a different quality, not given to our current research methods in western science at this time. Our Soul-Self is our Essence, our Greater Self vibrating at a faster, finer frequency. When we are at home in our Soul Self, we feel harmony, peace. Our personality's self, which is our less creatively powerful self, is the self that can give us challenges if we have not "gotten it together", or found cohesiveness within our personality realm. The personality self is often fragmented to various degrees.

However, the Soul-Self is always WHOLE. The energy and wide open perspective of the Soul-Self can bring healing and cohesion to the patterns of the personality. The Soul-Self can more quickly bring healing to the chaos that is often present at the personality level of self. Such chaos can be present to such a degree that little or no sense of "togetherness", little or no sense of balance can be experienced. Ideally, since we are here on Earth with a physical body, with the personality which has endured many experiences, it is preferred that we find ourselves at both levels of selfhood. Personality and Soul.

I recommend that we tap into the Soul-Self for a sense of well-being and for freedom from fear. Fear can nearly always be found lurking in the personality's self. Fortunately our Soul-Self is beyond such chaotic or dense vibrations of energy. It is a place of peace and wise guidance. The Soul Self is certainly the best place to go for a vacation.

Areas of the brain operating from the male principle (linear or alleged "left brain thinking") will experience reality as separate or concrete PARTICLES or parts. Areas of the brain functioning from the female principle (alleged "right brain") experience and interpret reality as WAVES of energy in motion. When the brain's dual male/female modes are functioning as a conscious partnership, we may more easily experience heart/Soul-Self sovereignty over the often-challenging human condition.

The **A**ware, **B**alanced, **C**ohesive personality or psychological self is a healthy human's reflection of one's Soul-Self. Remember, our personality parts or patterns may experience various degrees of fragmentation at various times of stress, yet the Soul is always whole. Our personality can grow toward cohesion and harmony eventually reflecting, to a large degree, our Soul-Self.

We can learn to dance back and forth between these two types of our selfhood – human personality and Soul Self, aiming for the heart in our body where the dense physical body meets spaciousness and Soul infusion.

The Human Growth Process™ honors both realms. It honors linear developmental psychology from western science, all that has been learned from Dr. S. Freud up to the present time. The Human Growth Process™ also honors The Energy Paradigm (N. Ging, 2001) described in detail in my previous books. This is the paradigm of spacious energy in motion where nothing is carved in stone as it is akin to the Quantum realm – the realm of energy in motion.

One of the very best occurrences with the Human Growth Process™ is experiencing how one's own Soul Energy can transform dense energies in the human body. The dense energies come out of our personality realm. One can even make a headache disappear by taking the energy of Consciousness, our Soul's energy, into the epicenter of a headache and breathing into that headache. It is more complicated with a migraine headache, but other headaches respond beautifully. So do the contracted energies of negative emotions as we focus on these contracted, dense energies and breathe into them. The qualitatively different energies of our two natures is something that we can easily learn feel physically. Our Soul energy is spacious and brings a feeling of joyful spaciousness, peaceful spaciousness to the body. Our human, physical nature is more dense. When we are feeling a miserable emotional of fear or hate, for example, our body experiences contracted energy. As we allow the energy of the Light of our Essence, our Soul, to infuse our physical body, remarkable physical healing often occurs. At the very least well-being can be ours.

We seem to be designed to be self-healing beings, designed for growth and the experience of self-actualization at the personality level AND true liberation as we develop the habit of leading more frequently with our heart and Soul.

Summary: Basic Concepts of The Human Growth Process™

1. The Human Growth Process™ is the Practice of Balancing Realities.

2. The Human Growth Process™ is based on a Unified Theory of Self™ (as put forth in Chapter Six) and also in more detail in *Simplifying The Road To Wholeness (2001)*

3. The Human Growth Process™ honors *both:*

   a. linear developmental psychology based on western science and

   b. the Energy Paradigm (N.Ging, 2001)

4. The Human Growth Process™ teaches individuals who wish to evolve (and therapists who may be supporting individuals in this growth process while calling forth the therapist's own evolution) how to clarify their identity by **re-defining themselves as living in two qualitatively different realities and having two qualitatively different conditions:**

   i) Wholeness, our *primary identity* (which can also be called our Complete Condition, Our

Greater/Larger Self, Our Soul, Our Holy/ Whole Condition, even Our Divine Condition, ONEness) AND ALSO

ii) The Human Condition, which is known herein as our *secondary condition.*

5. The Human Growth Process™ uses the Energy of Consciousness which is essentially emotionally neutral Awareness without judgement. This Energy of Consciousness for the observation of physical experience and thoughts can include the knowledge of electrical circuits in the body, as in Chinese Medicine, to transform limiting and disturbing patterns.

6. The Human Growth Process™ defines pathology (dysfunction or emotional illness) as the degree to which extreme patterns or parts, fragments of our Human Condition have moved into the foreground causing one to lose balance and forget one's primary identity of Wholeness.

7. Wholistic human growth work teaches that the two conditions, a) Wholeness and b) The Human Condition are not merely concepts, they are distinct qualities of energy that can be experienced, actually felt in the body.

8. The Human Growth Process™ teaches us that greater comfort is experienced when the energy of spaciousness/Consciousness is directed into the sometimes dense, contracted energies of aspects of our human condition or patterns/parts of our personality. Greater peace is known and felt when we experience the energy of our own heart's domain.

By Kevin Ging
Copyright 1995

REFERENCES

Amen, D., (1998) *Change your Brain, Change Your Life*, New York: Times Books.

Assagioli, R. (1973) *The Act of Will*, New York: Penguin.

Bohm, D., (1988) audio cassette "Parts Of A Whole" Boulder, CO: Soundstrue/New Dimensions.

Breiling, B. (1996) *Light Years Ahead*, Tiburon, CA: Light Years Ahead Publishing.

Capra, F., (1975) *The Tao Of Physics*, Boulder, CO: Shambhala.

Cambell, J,. (1989) videotape "The Transformation of Myth," Wm Free Productions.

Childre, D., and Martin, H. (1999) *The HeartMath Solution*, HarperSanFrancisco.

Ging, N.S.B., (2001) *Simplifying the Road to Wholeness*, Xlibris

Ging, N.S.B., (2016) *Knowing Wholeness; Through Poetry and Imagery*, Balboa Press

Hanson, R, PhD. and Mendius, R., M.D. (2009) *Buddha's Brain; The Practical Neuroscience of Happiness, Love and Wisdom*

Kohut, H. (1971) *Analysis Of The Self*, New York: International University Press.

Kramer, S. and Akhtar, S., (1994) *Mahler and Kohut*, Northvale, NY: Aronson.

Levinson D., (1978) *Seasons Of a Man's Life*, New York:Balentine, Ch. 14 and 15

Marcel, G. (1956) *The Philosophy of Existentialism*, New York:Philosophy Library

Mowrer, O.H. (1961) *The Crisis In Psychiatry and Religion*, Princeton, N..J.:D.VanNostrand.

Pearsall, Paul (1998) *The Heart's Code*, New York:Broadway Books.

Schwartz, R. (1995) *Internal Family Systems Therapy*, New York: Guilford Press.

Shapiro, F. (1995) *Eye Movement Desensitization And Reprocessing*, New York:Gilford.

Stone, H. and Winkelman, S. (1985) *Embracing Our Selves*, Marina del Rey, CA:Devorss & Co.

Theresa of Avila (1979)*The Interior Castle*. Trans. K.Kavanaugh and O. Rodriguez. New York:Paulist Press

Wagner, J. (1986) Stage Play *"The Search for Signs of Intelligent Life in the Universe*

Printed in the United States
By Bookmasters